All About Sports

All About
FOOTBALL

BY MATT DOEDEN

Consultant:
Craig R. Coenen, PhD
Professor of History
Mercer County Community College
West Windsor, New Jersey

CAPSTONE PRESS
a capstone imprint

A+ Books are published by Capstone Press,
1710 Roe Crest Drive, North Mankato, Minnesota 56003
www.capstonepub.com

Library of Congress Cataloging-in-Publication Data
Doeden, Matt.
   All about football / by Matt Doeden.
      pages cm. – (A+ books. all about sports)
   Includes bibliographical references and index.
   Summary: "Explains the game of football, including the game's
goals, positions, basic rules, and other points of interest"—
Provided by publisher.
   ISBN 978-1-4914-1995-3 (library binding)
   ISBN 978-1-4914-2172-7 (eBook PDF)
1. Football—Juvenile literature. I. Title.
   GV950.7.D628 2015
   796.33—dc23   2014027835

Editorial Credits
Brenda Haugen, editor; Sarah Bennett, designer; Eric Gohl,
media researcher; Katy LaVigne, production specialist

Photo Credits
Corbis: Bettmann, 8 (top); Dreamstime: Lawrence Weslowski
Jr., 15 (top); Getty Images: Sports Imagery/Ronald C. Modra,
26 (bottom right), Tony Tomsic, 26 (bottom left); Library of
Congress: 6–7 (all), 26 (top); Newscom: Cal Sport Media/Louis
Lopez, 18, Future Image/Imago sportfotodienst, 28–29, Icon
SMI/Andrew Richardson, 27, Icon SMI/Dustin Bradford, 16, Icon
SMI/MSA, 27 (top), Icon SMI/TMB, 13 (top), MCT/Ron Jenkins,
17, Qi Heng Xinhua News Agency, 28 (top), ZUMA Press/Paul
Childs, 10; Shutterstock: Adam Derewecki, 24–25, Amy Myers,
32, Aspen Photo, 4, 5, 9, 11 (inset), 15 (bottom), 21, bestv,
30–31, Beto Chagas, 22 (left), C_Eng-Wong Photography, 20,
Daniel Padavona, 14, Digital Storm, 1, Illustratiostock, 24 (left),
25 (top), JeepFoto, 16–17 (background), Mark Herreid, 11 (top),
Pete Saloutos, cover, 2–3, Richard Paul Kane, 8 (bottom), 12, 13
(bottom), 19, Susan Leggett, 22–23, winui, 18 (background)

Design Elements: Shutterstock

Note to Parents, Teachers, and Librarians
This All About Football book uses full color photographs and a
nonfiction format to introduce the concept of football. All About
Football is designed to be read aloud to a pre-reader or to be
read independently by an early reader. Photographs help listeners
and early readers understand the text and concepts discussed.
The book encourages further learning by including the following
sections: Table of Contents, Glossary, Read More, Internet Sites,
and Index. Early readers may need assistance using these features.

Printed in the United States of America in North Mankato, Minnesota.
102014   008482CGS15

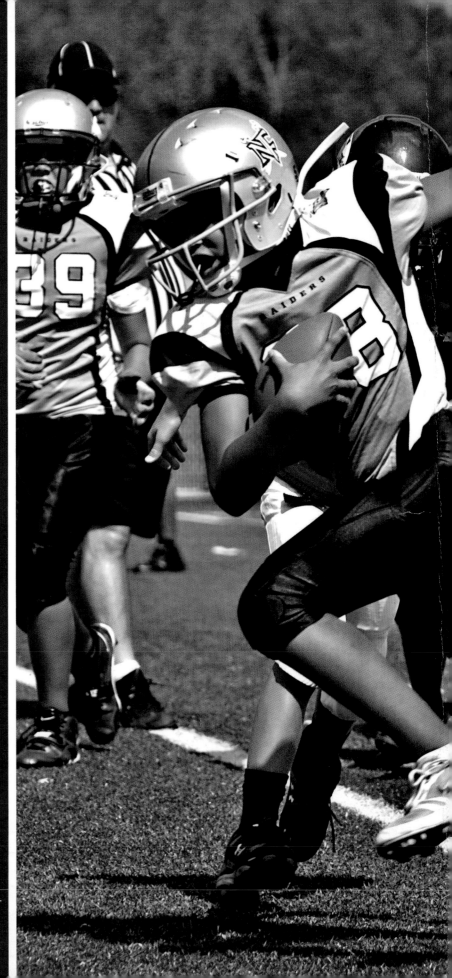

TABLE OF CONTENTS

TOUCHDOWN!

The quarterback throws a long pass. A receiver leaps and grabs the ball. His feet land in the **end zone** before he falls out of bounds.

Touchdown!

Long passes are part of what makes football so exciting.

end zone—an area at each end of a football field

touchdown—a six-point score in a football game

5

HISTORY

Football has been around since at least the 1860s. It started out as a mix of soccer and rugby. It looked very different from today's game.

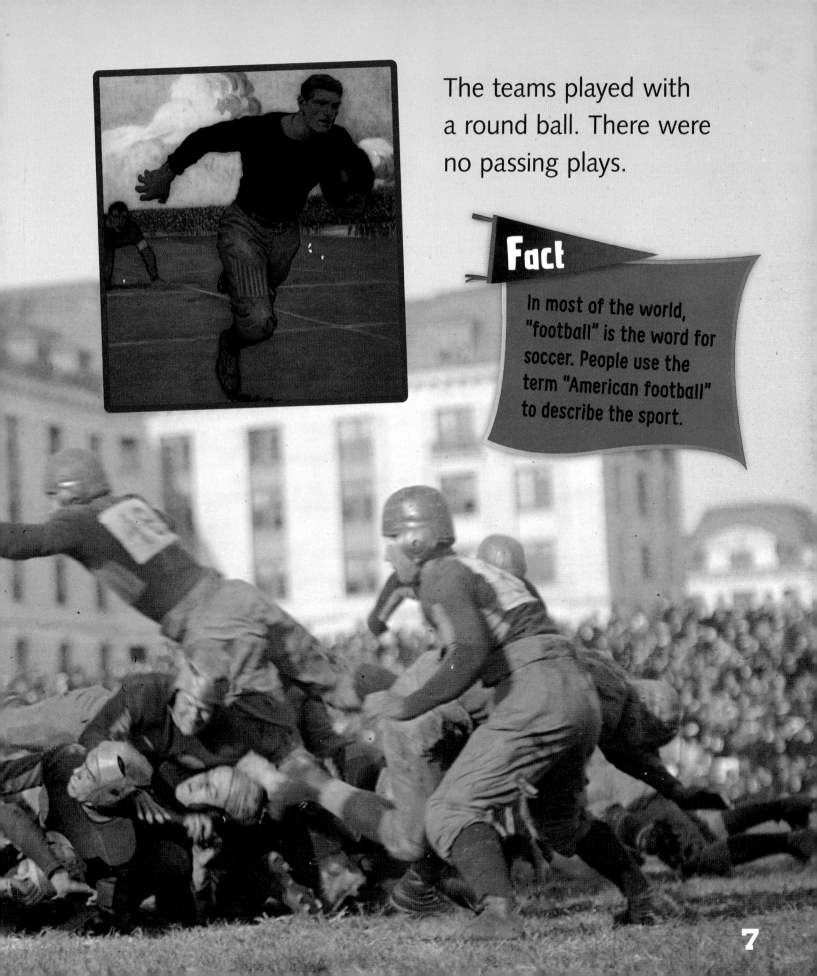

The teams played with a round ball. There were no passing plays.

A CHANGING GAME

The game changed in 1878. Former athlete Walter Camp wrote a new rule book. Camp allowed just 11 players per side. He created a **line of scrimmage**. This line separates the **offense** and **defense** before each play.

Walter Camp

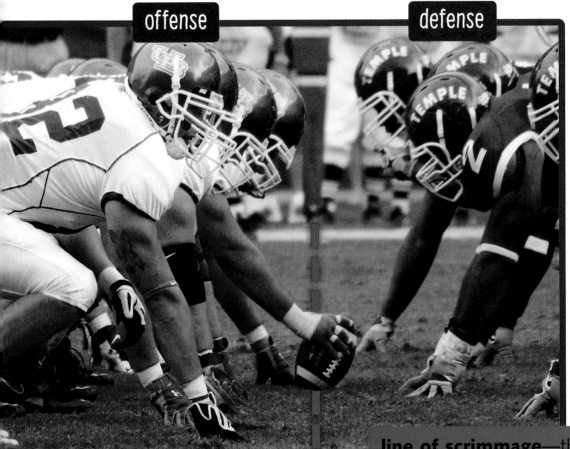

offense

defense

line of scrimmage

line of scrimmage—the imaginary line across a football field that goes out from where the football lies before a play begins

offense—the part of a football team whose main job is to score points

defense—the part of a football team whose main job is to stop the opponent from scoring

The forward pass was invented in the early 1900s. This exciting play helped the sport grow.

SCORING POINTS

Football is a clash between offense and defense.
The offense tries to score points. Getting the
ball into the end zone is a touchdown.

Kicking the ball through the **goalpost** is a **field goal**.

The defense can score points too. Tackling a player in his own end zone is a **safety**.

goalpost—a post that marks each end of the field; players get points for getting the ball through the goalpost

field goal—a play in which the ball is kicked through the goalpost for three points

safety—a two-point score made when an opposing player is tackled in his own end zone

Touchdown: 6 points

Field goal: 3 points

Safety: 2 points

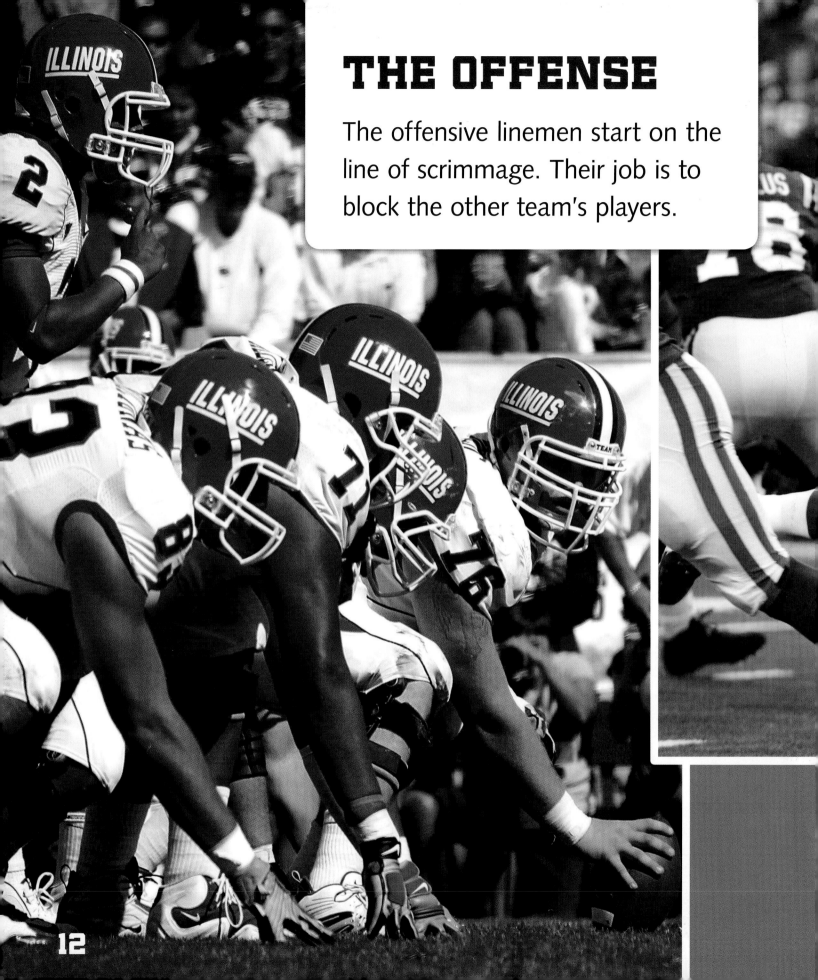

THE OFFENSE

The offensive linemen start on the line of scrimmage. Their job is to block the other team's players.

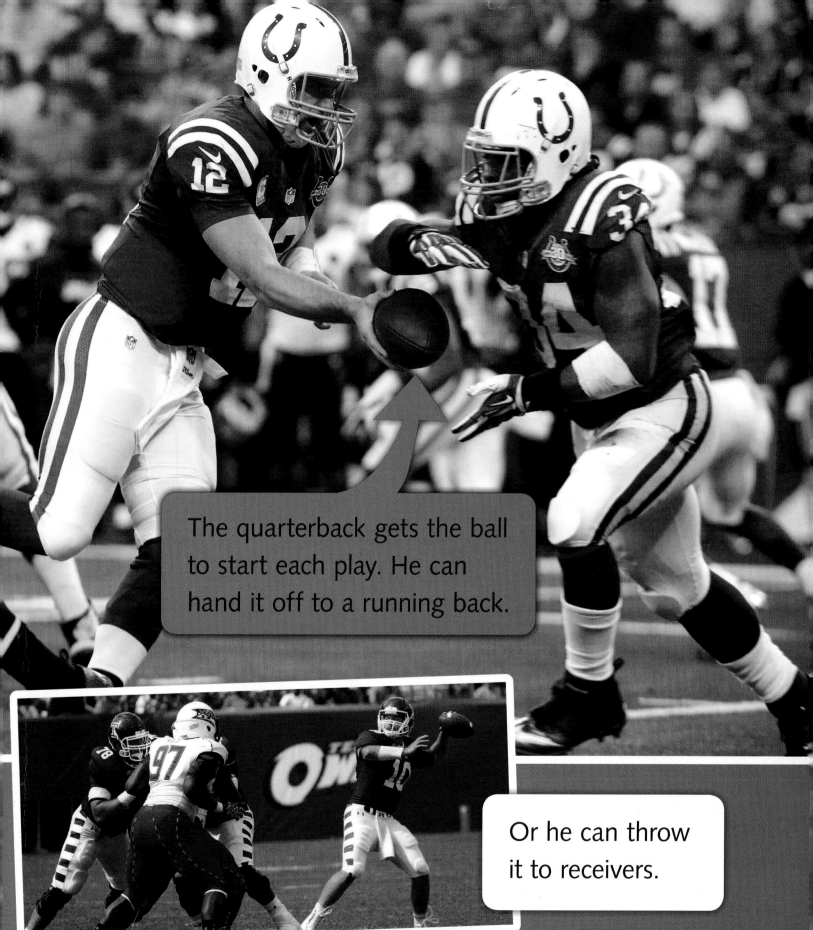

The quarterback gets the ball to start each play. He can hand it off to a running back.

Or he can throw it to receivers.

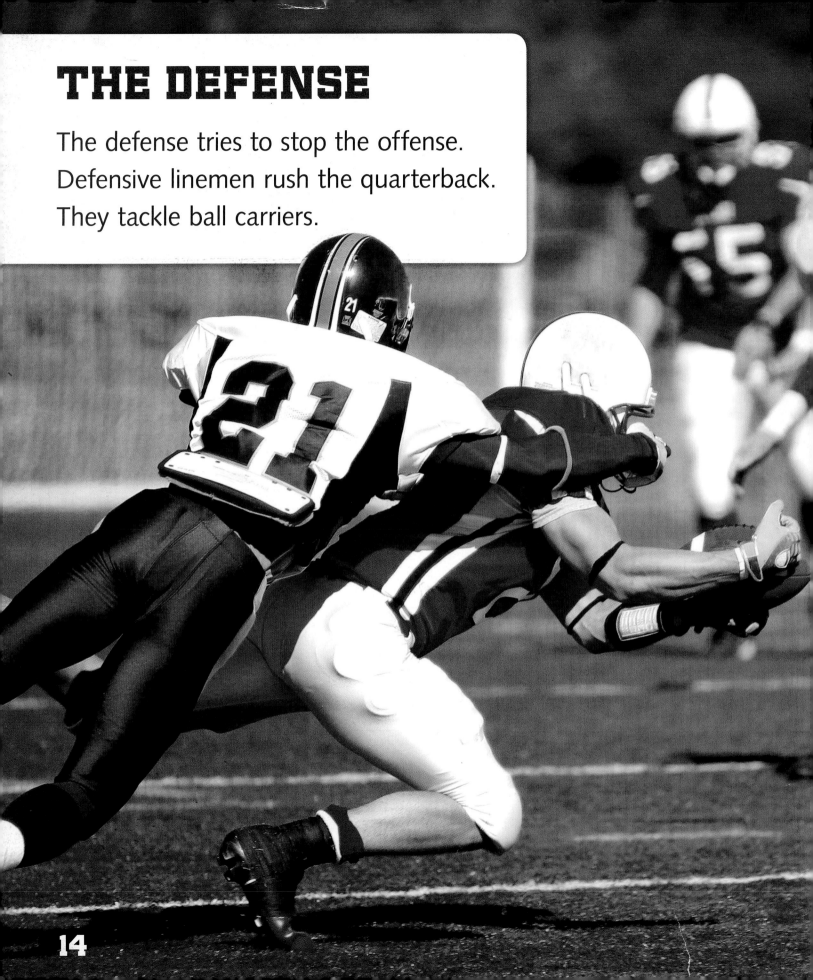

THE DEFENSE

The defense tries to stop the offense.
Defensive linemen rush the quarterback.
They tackle ball carriers.

The linebackers roam behind the line of scrimmage.

The defensive backs cover the other team's receivers.

DOWN AND DISTANCE

The offense has four plays to move the ball at least 10 yards. Each play is called a down.

Officials measure to see if a team got a first down. One official signals that the team is a little short of the first down.

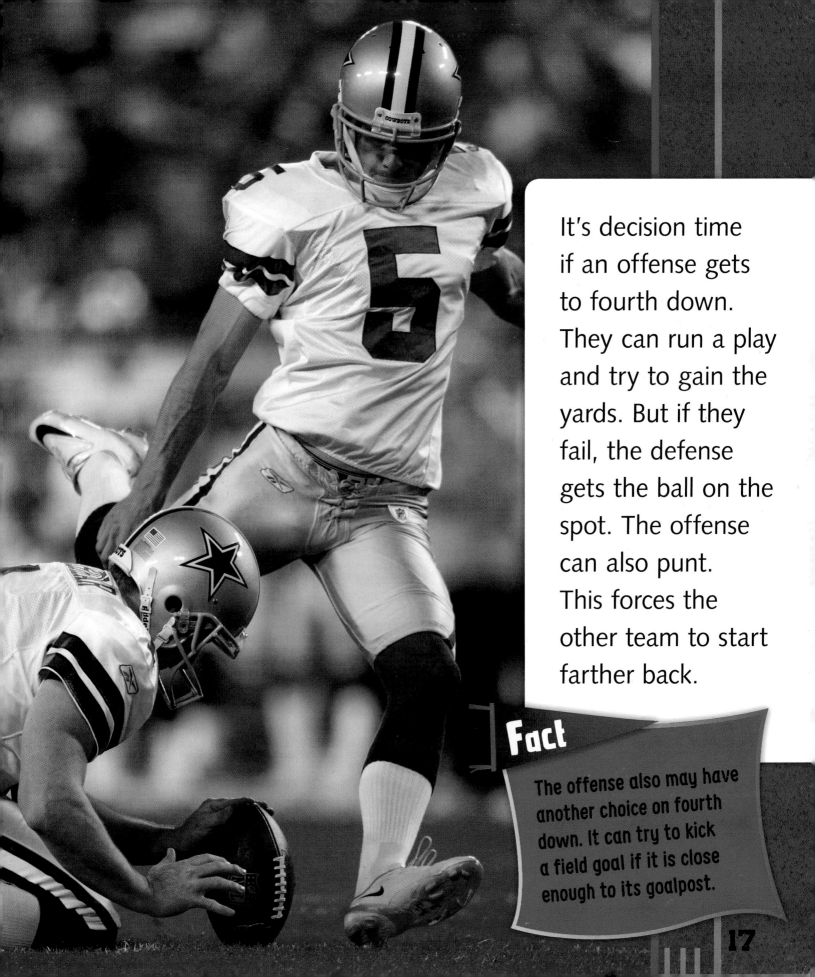

It's decision time if an offense gets to fourth down. They can run a play and try to gain the yards. But if they fail, the defense gets the ball on the spot. The offense can also punt. This forces the other team to start farther back.

Fact

The offense also may have another choice on fourth down. It can try to kick a field goal if it is close enough to its goalpost.

FOUR QUARTERS

The teams battle for four quarters. Halftime comes at the end of the second quarter. The team with more points at the end of the game wins.

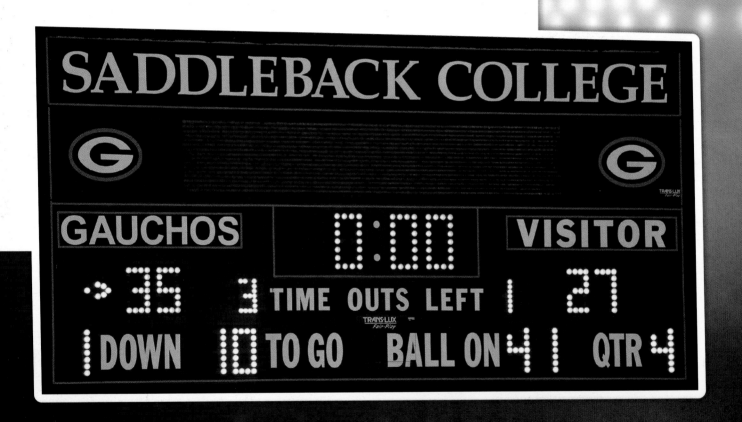

SADDLEBACK COLLEGE

GAUCHOS   0:00   VISITOR

35   3 TIME OUTS LEFT 1   27

1 DOWN   10 TO GO   BALL ON 41   QTR 4

TRANS·LUX
Fair-Play

Referees help to run a football game. They call penalties when players break rules.

penalty—a punishment for breaking the rules

19

THE BALL

A football game starts with a football.

Modern footballs are oval. They have pointed ends.

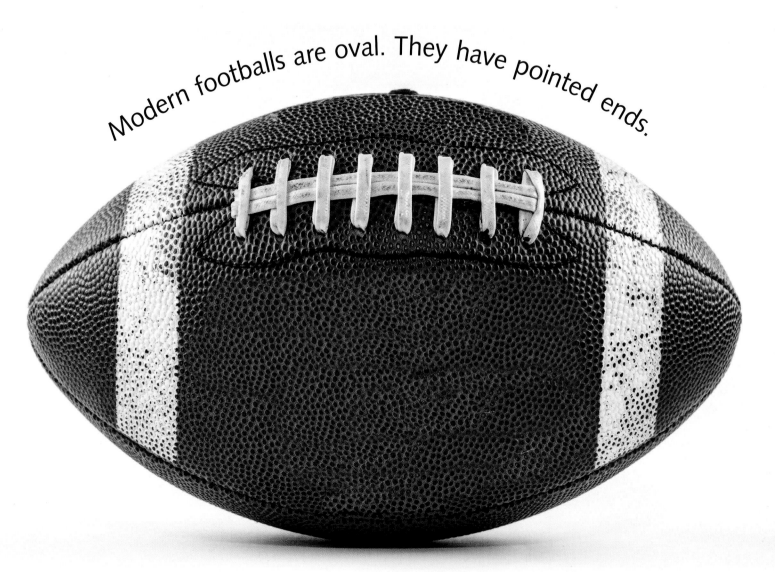

They are made of leather.

Fact

An NFL football weighs about 15 ounces (425 grams).

Laces help players grip the ball.

SAFETY GEAR

Smash! Crash! Thud!

Football is a rough game. Players leap, spin, and tackle each other. They need protection.

Strong plastic helmets protect their heads. Pads cover their shoulders, thighs, and knees.

THE FIELD

A football field is 100 yards (91 meters) long. Each yard is marked with a line.

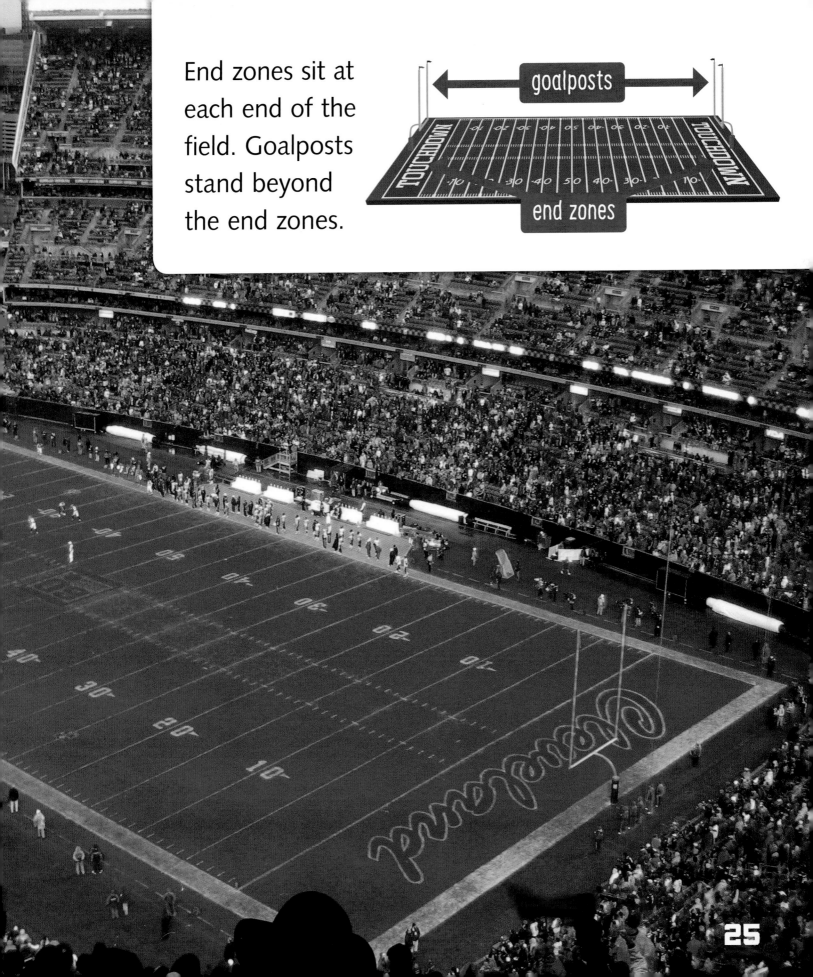

End zones sit at each end of the field. Goalposts stand beyond the end zones.

goalposts

TOUCHDOWN

TOUCHDOWN

end zones

THE NFL

The best football players hope to play in the NFL. Legends such as Red Grange, Johnny Unitas, and Walter Payton built the sport.

Red Grange

Walter Payton

Johnny Unitas

Fact
The National Football League (NFL) started in 1920.

Stars such as Calvin Johnson and J.J. Watt thrill fans today.

Calvin Johnson

J.J. Watt

27

THE SUPER BOWL

The biggest goal for NFL players is winning the Super Bowl. It is the NFL's championship game. Few players get the chance to hoist the Super Bowl trophy. But those who do never forget it.

GLOSSARY

defense—the part of a football team whose main job is to stop the opponent from scoring points

end zone—an area at each end of a football field

field goal—a play in which the ball is kicked through the goalpost for three points

goalpost—a post that marks each end of the field; players get points for getting the ball through the goalpost

line of scrimmage—the imaginary line across a football field that goes out from where the football lies before a play begins

offense—the part of a football team whose main job is to score points

penalty—a punishment for breaking the rules

safety—a two-point score made when an opposing player is tackled in his own end zone

touchdown—a six-point score in a football game

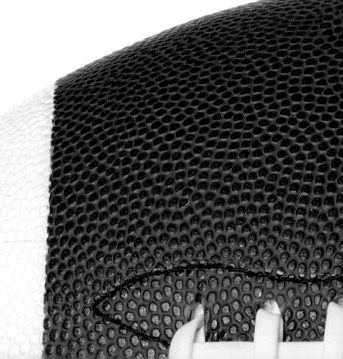

READ MORE

Nelson, Robin. *Football Is Fun!* Sports Are Fun!
Minneapolis: Lerner Publications Co., 2014.

Storden, Thom. *Amazing Football Records.* Epic Sports
Records. North Mankato, Minn: Capstone Press, 2015.

Weakland, Mark. *Football ABC.* Sports Illustrated Kids
Rookie Books. North Mankato, Minn.: Capstone Press, 2013.

INTERNET SITES

FactHound offers a safe, fun way to find Internet
sites related to this book. All of the sites on
FactHound have been researched by our staff.

Here's all you do:
Visit www.facthound.com
Type in this code: 9781491419953

Super-cool stuff!

Check out projects, games and lots more at
www.capstonekids.com

INDEX